ASSESSING YOUR CHILD'S PROGRE

GW00993648

Testing and assessment in the National Curriculum

Pupils between the ages of 7 and 11 (Years 3–6) cover Key Stage 2 of the National Curriculum. In May of their final year of Key Stage 2 (Year 6) all pupils take written National Tests (commonly known as SATs) in the three most important subjects: English, Mathematics and Science. Your child may already have taken some National Tests at the end of Key Stage 1 (Year 2). These will have been in number, shape and space, reading, writing, handwriting and spelling.

At the end of Key Stage 1, your child will have been awarded a National Curriculum level for each subject tested. When your child eventually takes the Key Stage 2 tests, he or she again will be awarded a level. On average, pupils are expected to advance one level for every two years they are at school. The target for pupils at the end of Key Stage 1 is Level 2. By the end of Key Stage 2, four years later, the target is Level 4. The table below will show you how your child should progress.

		7 years	11 years
■ Exceptional performance	Level 6		■
	Level 5		■
■ Exceeded targets for age group	Level 4	■	■
■ Achieved targets for age group	Level 3	■	■
	Level 2	■	■
■ Working towards targets for age group	Level 1	■	■

Assessing your child's progress throughout Key Stage 2 of the National Curriculum

The aim of the Letts Assessment books is to help you monitor your child's progress in English, Mathematics and Science throughout Key Stage 2. There are four books for each subject – one for each year, starting with 7–8 year olds. The questions in the books become progressively harder with each year, so that for 10–11 year olds, the questions will be at a level similar to the Key Stage 2 National Tests.

After completing a book, your child will have a score which you will be able to interpret using the progress indicator provided. This will give you a guide to the level at which your child is working.

Using this book to assess your child's progress in Science

This book contains four basic features:

Questions: 31 questions, arranged in order of difficulty as follows:
15 at Level 2 (pages 1–17)
16 at Level 3 (pages 18–39)

Answers: showing acceptable responses and marks

Note to Parent: giving advice on what your child should be doing and how to help

Progress Chart: showing you how to interpret your child's marks to arrive at a level

- Your child should not attempt to do all the questions in the book in one go. Try setting ten questions at a time. If your child does not understand a question, you might want to explain it. Although the questions in this book are not meant to constitute a formal test, you should encourage your child to answer as many as possible without help. Read the questions to your child if you think it will help.

- When your child has completed the questions, turn to the Answer section at the back of the book. Using the recommended answers, award your child the appropriate mark or marks for each question. In the margin of each question page, there are small boxes. These are divided in half with the marks available for that question at the bottom, and a blank at the top for you to fill in your child's score.

- Collate your child's marks on the grid on page 46. Then add them up. Once you have the total, turn to page 40 at the front of the Answer section and look at the Progress Chart to determine your child's level.

- Work through the answers with your child, using the Note to Parent to help give advice, correct mistakes and explain problems.

Equipment your child will need for this book

All your child needs are a pen or pencil for writing, and a pencil for drawing. Your child may also like to have a rubber for changing answers. Where lines have to be drawn, they can be drawn either with a ruler or freehand, whichever your child feels most comfortable with.

1   Jo went for a walk through the woods.

These are
the animals
Jo saw.

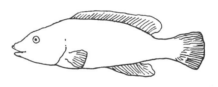

a
> One animal lives in the pond.
> Draw a line from that animal to the pond.

1

Q1a

b
> One animal lives in a nest in the tree.
> Draw a line from that animal to the nest.

1

Q1b

Here are some leaves that Jo collected.

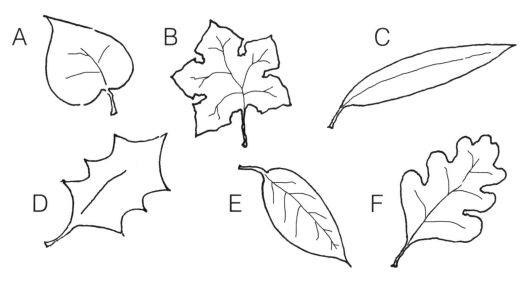

Jo put the leaves into groups.

2

Q1c

Finish putting the leaves into groups. Write down the letter of each leaf in the boxes below. One has been done for you.

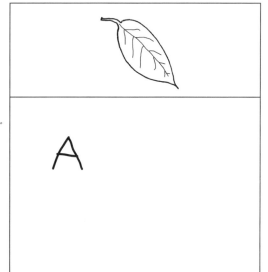

A

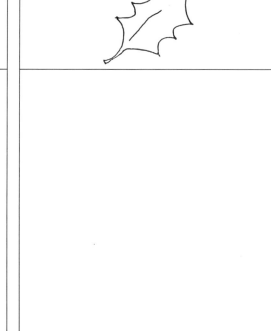

2   Tim and his mum had been shopping.

Tim put some of the shopping into a group. He made a group of things that could bend easily.

a

> Put the rest of the shopping into **two** groups.
> Make one group of things that are liquids.
> Make one group of things that are solids.

2

Q2a

Tim poured some orange juice into a dish and put it into the freezer. The next day Tim took the dish of orange juice out of the freezer.

b

> Tick ✓ one box that tells you what the orange juice was like.

1

Q2b

It could be poured into a cup. ☐

It was in one hard piece. ☐

It could bend easily. ☐

3   Look at the pictures of things that make sound.

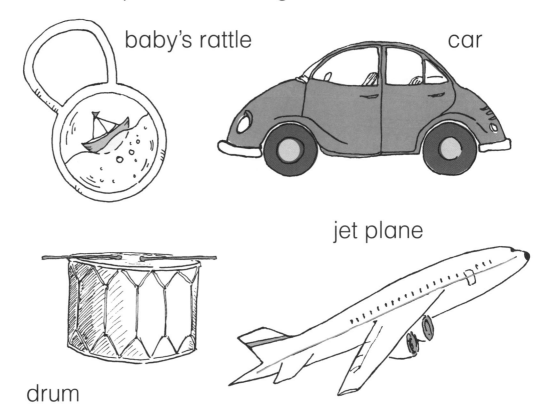

baby's rattle

car

jet plane

drum

1
Q3a

a   Which thing can make the loudest sound?

1
Q3b

b   Which thing makes the quietest sound?

1
Q3c

c   Which thing must be hit to make a sound?

4   Peter's parents are having a new garage built next to their house. The garage is built of different materials.

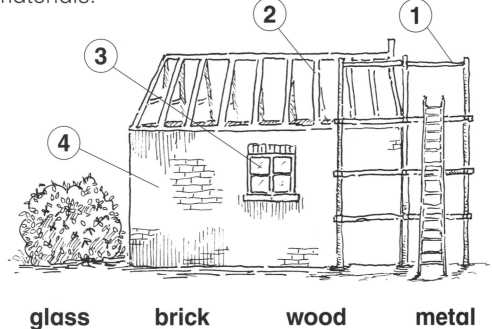

glass   brick   wood   metal

a   Draw lines to match each number to the correct material.

Q4a

Some things about metal and wood are the same and some are different.

b   Place a tick ✓ or a cross ✗ in each box in the table.

Q4b

	strong	burns	rots
metal			
wood			

5   Kerry had a puppy for her birthday.

a   Tick ✓ **two** boxes which show what Kerry must give to the puppy to keep it alive.

| food | kennel | light | water |

b   Choose words from the list to complete the sentences.

body   diet   grow   reproduce

Kerry's puppy is very small but it will .... into a big dog.

To keep the puppy healthy it must have a good ....

Letts

6   Bob rolled some things down a ramp. He noticed that some things rolled down the ramp faster than others.

These are the things that Bob rolled down the ramp.

a ball   a pencil   a shoe

a | Bob started a list to show which things rolled down the ramp fastest. Finish the list by writing in the names of the things. |

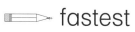 fastest   .... ball ....

....

slowest   ....

b | What could Bob have done to make the ball roll down the ramp even faster? |

 ....

....

2
Q6a

1
Q6b

7

7   Orange drink is sold in glass bottles,
plastic bottles, aluminium cans
and cardboard cartons.

 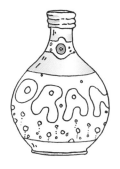  

aluminium   glass   cardboard   plastic

a   Put each material in the correct boxes.

see-through	burns when hot	melts when hot

b   Orange drink is **not** sold in containers made
from silver. Tick ✓ the best reason for this.

 too shiny ☐

too light ☐

too heavy ☐

too expensive ☐

8   The picture shows living
    and non-living things.

glass    dog

a   Circle the **two** things the dog can do but the glass cannot do.

grow   reproduce   shine   smash

b   Underline the **three** things the dog must have to keep him alive.

air   collar   food   music   play   water

c   Tick ✓ **one** box for each description of the glass or dog. One has been done for you.

	glass	dog
is shiny	✓	
is see-through		
is soft to touch		
is living		
is non-living		

9 Look at the pictures of some things which make light.

candle

desk lamp

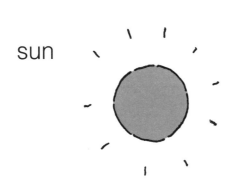

sun

traffic lights

a

Circle the brightest light.

b

Which thing can make light in three different colours?

c

Which **two** things need electricity to work?

10   This picture shows a drag racing car at the end of the race.

> Choose words from the list to complete the sentences.

2

Q10

faster   pulls   pushes   slower

The open parachute .... on the racing car.

This makes it get ....

11   Look at this picture of plants living by a pond.

a   (Circle) **two** things that all these plants need to stay alive and healthy.

    fields   light   soil   walls   water

b   In the spring the pond has tadpoles in it. (Circle) the most important thing tadpoles must have to grow and change into frogs.

    food   light   shelter   warmth

12   Look at the pictures.

clockwork toy

fridge

gas cooker

television

a   Circle **two** pictures that show things that need electricity to work.

b   Write down the name of another thing that needs electricity to work.

....

13   Matthew is going camping in Scotland.

Sam is going to a hotel in Spain.

Look at these pictures of the clothes they might take on holiday.

sandals

shorts

wellington boots

scarf

T-shirt

sun hat

trousers

woolly hat

swimming trunks

jumper

gloves

sun glasses

LEVEL 2

MARKS

a

What should Matthew put in his rucksack?

3
Q13a

....

....

....

....

....

....

b

What should Sam put in his suitcase?

3
Q13b

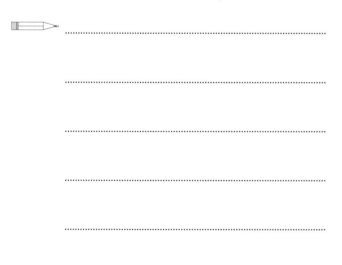

....

....

....

....

....

....

14 Look at these animals.

Polar bears have thick fur to keep them warm.

Penguins swim and catch fish in cold water.

Snakes are cold-blooded and live in a warm climate.

Seals feed on fish.

4
Q14

Write the name of each animal under the place it would live.

a

b

✏ ....

✏ ....

c

d

✏ ....

✏ ....

15 a

How would you make a sound on these instruments?

3

Q15a

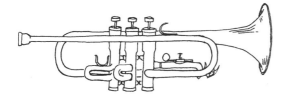

a trumpet

a guitar

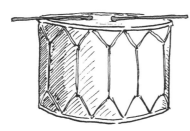

a drum

b

Which of these instruments can make the loudest sound? Circle your choice.

1

Q15b

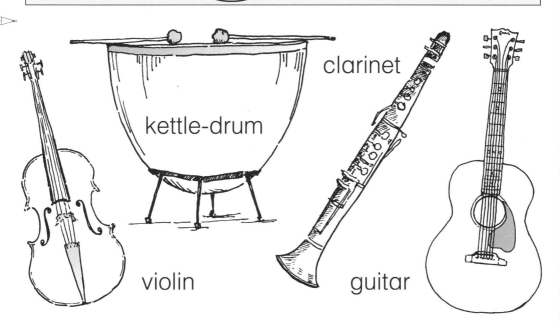

clarinet

kettle-drum

violin

guitar

16 Sally bought a new plant from the garden centre.

....

....

a What are the names of the parts of the plant?
Write in **leaf**, **stem** and **flower**.

b Draw lines to match the words to the pictures.

| Two weeks later, growing well. | Two months later, if Sally never waters it. | One week later, if Sally forgets to water it. |

17 Jane had some baby chickens and did not know which type of feed was best. She fed one baby chicken on Mixture A and the other baby chicken on Mixture B.

baby chicken fed on Mixture A

baby chicken fed on Mixture B

Jane weighed the baby chickens every ten days. This is what Jane wrote down.

age of baby chickens	0 days	10 days	20 days	30 days
baby chicken fed on Mixture A	42g	150g	320g	750g
baby chicken fed on Mixture B	42g	213g	650g	1100g

a How much did the baby chickens weigh when they were born?

_____ g

1

Q17a

19

MARKS

b How much did the baby chickens weigh when they were 20 days old?

 baby chicken fed on Mixture A .... g

 baby chicken fed on Mixture B.. g

c A 30 day old baby chicken usually weighs 1000g. Which mixture of food do you think Jane should use to feed her baby chickens?

 ....

d Tick ✓ the best ending to this sentence.

Jane chose this mixture of food because . . .

 ☐ . . . it could be poured into a cup.

☐ . . . it gave the chickens the best weight.

☐ . . . it was easy to pour into the dish.

e Write down **one** other thing Jane would need to give her baby chickens to keep them healthy.

....

18 As Jane walked around the farm she saw lots of different things.

Jane made a list of things to show which were living and which were non-living.

a

Tick ✓ **one** box for each thing to show if it is living or non-living.

4
Q18a

	living	**non-living**
tractor	☐	☐
duck	☐	☐
tree	☐	☐
barn	☐	☐

b

Write down **two** things the living things can do that the non-living things cannot do.

2
Q18b

1 ....

2 ....

19   Jo is trying to pick up a duck with a magnetic fishing rod at the fair.

a   Circle the duck that Jo will pick up with the magnet on the end of her rod.

1
Q19a

b   Tick ✔ the material that Jo could also pick up with the magnet on the end of her rod.

1
Q19b

iron   ☐

wood   ☐

plastic   ☐

glass   ☐

20   Look at the picture.

Choose words from the list to complete the sentences.

burn   cold   heat   melt   metal   rubber

➡ Saucepans are made of ....

➡ This is used because it is a material that lets

.... pass through it.

➡ Wood is not used because it would ....

23

MARKS

21 Jane and Emily both have dolls' houses with lights which work in every room. The lights work from a battery.

Emily's
dolls' house

Jane's
dolls' house

2

Q21a

a Jane's lights are not as bright as Emily's. Can you think of **two** reasons for this?

 1 ....

....

 2 ....

....

Emily has made another dolls' house with two rooms from a shoe box. She has made a circuit to light a lamp in each room.

This is the circuit.

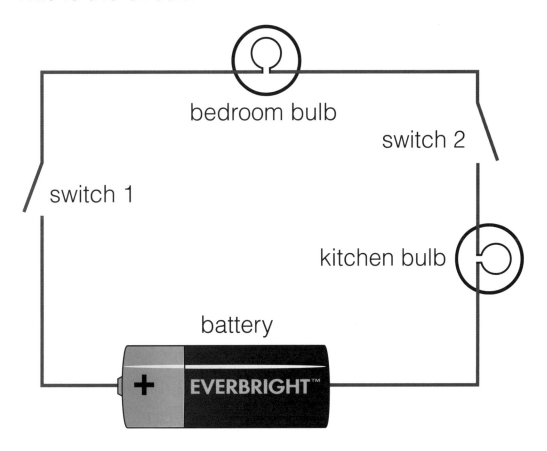

bedroom bulb

switch 2

switch 1

kitchen bulb

battery

EVERBRIGHT™

b How many switches have to be pressed to light the bedroom bulb?

1

Q21b

c How many switches have to be pressed to light the kitchen bulb?

1

Q21c

22 Fred was cleaning out his garage.

newspaper

rock   plastic bags

iron nail

aluminium can

Fred grouped the things he found by their properties.

> Write the names of each thing under the heading that best describes its properties. The first one has been done for you.

hard	bendy
aluminium can	

4
Q22

23 Look at the picture of a racket hitting a squash ball.

a   Draw an arrow on the picture to show which way the ball will move.

1
Q23a

b   What will happen to the speed of the ball as it moves away from the racket?

1
Q23b

c   A force is acting on the ball. What has the force done to the shape of the ball?

1
Q23c

24   Look at the picture of a rock pool.

Limpets are animals which live in shells.

They feed on small plants which cover the rocks in the pools left when the tide goes out.

Limpets stick firmly to rocks with a very strong "foot". It is almost impossible to detach a limpet from a rock.

a

> What makes a limpet well suited to living in a rock pool?

1

Q24a

Young limpets do not have shells. They swim to new rock pools to find food.

b

> Not all rock pools have limpets in them. Can you think of a reason for this?

1

Q24b

25   The picture shows Peter's new bicycle.

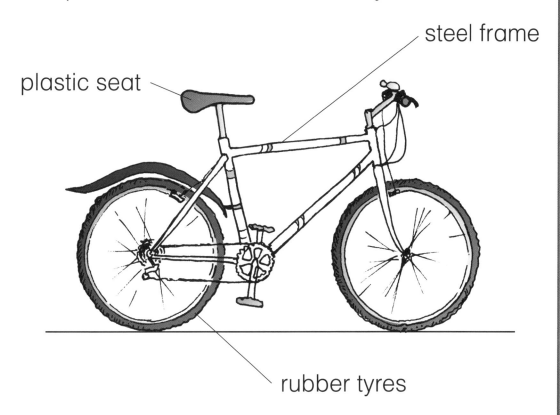

steel frame

plastic seat

rubber tyres

Many different materials were used to make it.

Tick ✔ the box which explains why bicycle makers use different materials.

a   The frame of the bicycle is made from **steel** because steel . . .

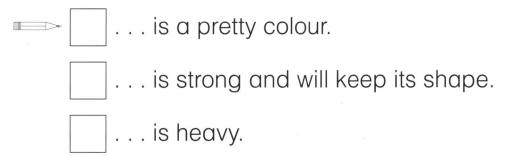

☐ . . . is a pretty colour.

☐ . . . is strong and will keep its shape.

☐ . . . is heavy.

1

Q25a

MARKS

1

Q25b

b The seat is made from **plastic** because plastic . . .

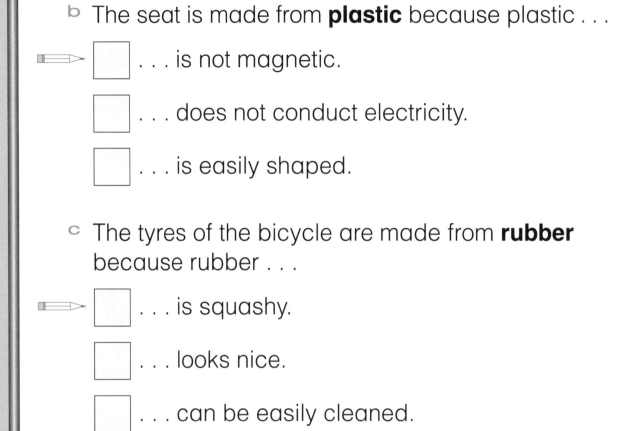

☐ . . . is not magnetic.

☐ . . . does not conduct electricity.

☐ . . . is easily shaped.

1

Q25c

c The tyres of the bicycle are made from **rubber** because rubber . . .

☐ . . . is squashy.

☐ . . . looks nice.

☐ . . . can be easily cleaned.

26 Bradley helped his mother to bake biscuits.

Before cooking,
the biscuit mixture was
soft, easily stirred and
a pale brown colour.

After cooking,
the biscuits were
hard and a dark
brown colour.

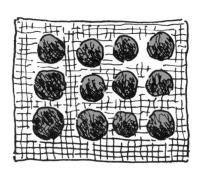

a

> Tick ✓ the sentence that describes why the
> biscuit mixture changed.

1

Q26a

The biscuit mixture was left for one hour. ☐

The biscuit mixture was put in a hot oven. ☐

Water was added to the biscuit mixture. ☐

Bradley put some orange juice into the freezer to make ice lollies. The next day he took the ice lollies out of the freezer. He ate one and left the other on the table.

The pictures show what happened to the ice lolly on the table after one hour.

ice lolly when taken from the freezer

ice lolly after one hour

b

Circle the word that describes what has happened to the ice lolly.

1

Q26b

frozen   **melted**   **mixed**

The ice lolly changed back to how it was before.

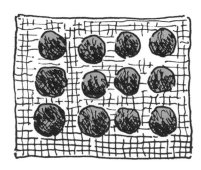

The biscuit mixture could not change back.

c

Tick ✓ **one** box for each of the changes to show if it can change back to how it was before or if it cannot change back.

3

Q26c

	can change back	cannot change back
baking cakes	☐	☐
making ice cubes	☐	☐
baking clay into bricks	☐	☐

27 Jane made some circuits using a battery, two wires and a bulb.

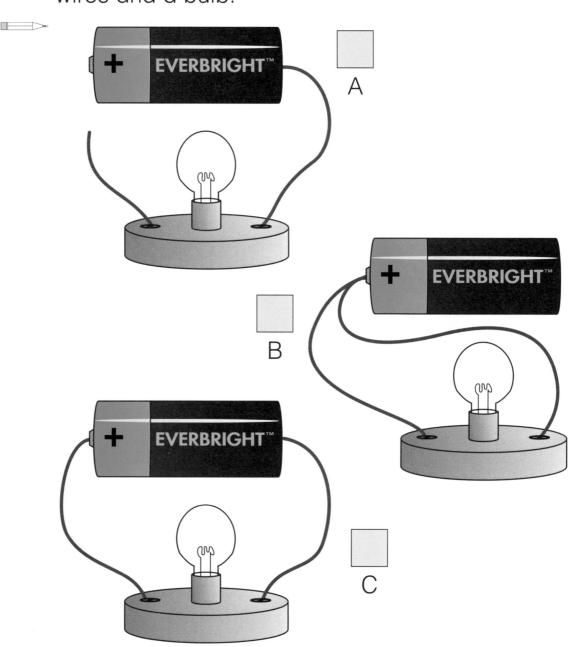

Only **one** circuit made the bulb light up.

a

Tick ✓ the box to show which circuit made the bulb light up.

Jane made three more circuits to try and make the bulb brighter. Here are the circuits Jane made.

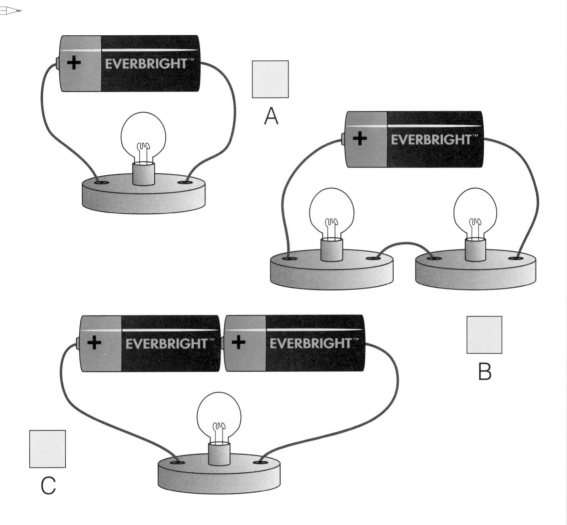

A

B

C

b
Tick ✓ the box to show which bulb was the brightest.

1
Q27b

c
Write down why this bulb was the brightest.

1
Q27c

28 Look at the picture of the children and their teacher in the playground.

John   Mary   Keith

The teacher blew the whistle.

a Circle the child who hears the loudest whistle sound.

b Explain why that child can hear it louder than the others.

....

....

29 The picture shows a car hitting a wall.

a | Will the car push or pull the wall?

1

Q29a

....

b | The force of the wall on the car changes the
   | car. Tick ✓ **two** boxes to show the changes the
   | force will make.

2

Q29b

changes its shape   ☐

slows it down   ☐

speeds it up   ☐

melts it   ☐

Letts

30 The table shows some properties of different materials.

material	property
glass	see-through
gold	shiny
iron	strong
plastic	can be moulded

Use the table to finish these sentences. The first one has been done for you.

A window is made of ___glass___ because it is ___see-through___ .

A nail is made of _____ because it is _____ .

A bucket is made of _____ because it _____ .

Jewellery is made of _____ because it is _____ .

3
Q30

31 The picture shows a battery and two bulbs.

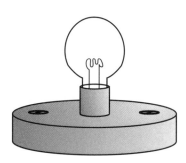

a What is the smallest number of wires you would need to join the bulbs to the battery so that they both light up? Choose from **1**, **2**, **3** or **4**.

1
Q31a

b Draw these wires on the picture to show how you could make the bulbs light up.

1
Q31b

c Tick ✓ **one** box to show what you could add to make the bulbs brighter.

1
Q31c

a second battery

a switch

a third bulb

- When marking your child's questions, remember that the answers given here are the answers the question-setter expects. You must look at your child's answers and judge whether they deserve credit.

- At this age, your child's spelling may show a number of errors. Do not mark any answer wrong because the words are misspelt. Read the word aloud and, if it sounds correct, award the mark. For example, 'ekwul' would be acceptable for 'equal'.

- When you go through the questions with your child, try to be positive. Look for good things that have been done in addition to showing where errors have been made.

- Enter your child's marks on the grid on page 46, and then refer to the table below to determine your child's level.

Progress Chart

Total marks scored	Progress made	Suggested action
30 or below	Your child's mark shows some knowledge and understanding of the skills associated with Level 2 work.	Identify areas of weakness from the early part of the test. Try to organise practical activities for your child to do at home to gain more experience.
31–50	Your child is confident in working with several concepts at Level 2.	Encourage your child to make models using electrical circuits and to practise grouping objects together to increase confidence with these skills.
51–70	Your child has mastered the fundamental science at Level 2 and is starting to grasp some higher level concepts.	Start to encourage your child to give simple explanations for everyday observations, such as why materials are suited to particular uses.
71–90	A mark in this range is typical of a child who is confident with Level 2 and has some of the skills associated with Level 3.	Identify areas of weakness from the second half of the book and try to give your child more practise with activities that reinforce these areas.
91 and above	Your child is displaying much of the skills, knowledge and understanding associated with Level 3 work.	Encourage your child to ask questions about everyday phenomena, and to seek explanations.

- A child at the end of Year 3 (7–8 year olds) should be, of the above statements, between the third and the fourth statements.

1 a Line drawn from the fish to the pond   *1 mark*
   b Line drawn from the bird to the nest   *1 mark*

Note to Parent

Encourage your child to draw a line all the way from the fish to the pond. If the line stops between the fish and rabbit, no marks are awarded.

   c A C E   B D F
     Award one mark for each correctly completed group   *2 marks*

Note to Parent

If your child groups the leaves differently, ask why he or she grouped them together this way. Explain about the shape of the leaves. You can improve your child's skill at grouping using collections of household objects and asking your child to put them into groups according to their shape, size or colour.

Total 4 marks

2 a Circle grouping together liquids: milk, pop and orange juice
     Circle grouping together solids: cheese, chocolate and biscuits
     Award one mark for each correct group of items   *2 marks*
   b It was in one hard piece.   *1 mark*

Note to Parent

Children working at Level 2 and above should be familiar with the effects of heating and cooling on everyday objects.

Total 3 marks

3 a   jet plane   b baby's rattle   c drum   *1 mark each*
                                                                   Total 3 marks

4 a 1 metal 2 wood   3 glass   4 brick   *1 mark each*
   b metal: tick strong, cross burns and rots   *2 marks*
     wood: tick burns and rots, cross strong   *2 marks*
     Award two marks for all correct; one mark for only two correct

Note to Parent

This question assesses whether or not your child can identify a range of common materials and can describe the similarities and differences between them.

Total 8 marks

5 a food and water   *1 mark each*
   b grow; diet   *1 mark each*
                                                           Total 4 marks

6 a faster: pencil   slowest: shoe   *1 mark each*
   b *Either* increase the slope of the ramp *or* push the ball with more force   *1 mark*
                                                           Total 3 marks

7 a see-through: glass, plastic   *1 mark*
     burns: plastic, cardboard   *1 mark*
     melts: plastic, aluminium, glass   *2 marks*
     Award two marks if all correct; one mark if only two correct

b too expensive   *1 mark*

This question assesses if your child can sort materials into groups on the basis of their properties.

Total 5 marks

8 a grow and reproduce   *1 mark each*

Note to Parent

Your child might assume this is the wrong answer because they are the first two in the list. Lists of words are usually in alphabetical order so it is quite common to have two answers together.

b air, food and water   *1 mark each*
c 'glass' boxes should be ticked for see-through and non-living   *1 mark each*
   'dog' boxes should be ticked for soft to touch and living   *1 mark each*

Note to Parent

Do not penalise incorrect answers unless both glass and dog boxes are ticked for one description. Then award nothing for that description.

Total 9 marks

9 a sun   b traffic lights   *1 mark each*
   c traffic lights and desk lamp   *1 mark each*
                                                                                             Total 4 marks

10 pulls; slower   *1 mark each*

Note to Parent

This question is assessing your child's understanding of how forces can be used to slow down an object.

Total 2 marks

11 a light and water   *1 mark each*
   b food   *1 mark*
                                                                                             Total 3 marks

12 a television and fridge   *1 mark each*
   b anything that uses electricity   *1 mark*

Note to Parent

This question is assessing whether your child knows which things work from electricity.

Total 3 marks

13 a jumper, woolly hat, scarf, trousers, wellington boots, gloves   *3 marks*
   b swimming trunks, T-shirt, sun hat, shorts, sandals, sun glasses   *3 marks*
      Award one mark for each two items in the correct place

Note to Parent

This question is assessing whether your child understands that some materials are better thermal insulators than others.

Total 6 marks

14 a snake   b seal   c penguin   d polar bear   *1 mark each*

Note to Parent

This question tests whether your child can match different living things to their habitats.

Total 4 marks

15 a trumpet: blow it   guitar: pluck it   drum: hit or bang it   *1 mark each*
b kettle-drum   *1 mark*

Note to Parent

Your child can learn how to make sounds and change the pitch and loudness using a simple home-made instrument. A rubber band stretched between two nails in a piece of wood is cheap and easy to make.

Total 4 marks

16 a   *3 marks*

flower
stem
leaf

Note to Parent

As well as knowing the names of the main parts of a plant shown in the picture, your child should also know about roots. Some children confuse the terms 'plant' and 'flower'. It is useful to help your child to appreciate that the term plant is a broad umbrella one and that flowers are the reproductive parts of the plant, some of which are brightly coloured to attract insects.

b growing well   two months   one week   *1 mark each*

Note to Parent

Water is essential for the growth and survival of plants. The effects of lack of water, as shown in the question, can be easily demonstrated at home, as can the effect of lack of light. Try putting a pot plant into a dark cupboard for a few weeks.

Total 6 marks

17 a 42g   *1 mark*
b mixture A: 320g   mixture B: 650g   *1 mark each*
c mixture B   *1 mark*
d it gave the chickens the best weight   *1 mark*
e water (accept warmth)   *1 mark*

Note to Parent

Your child is not expected to know about the growth of chickens specifically. This question is designed to assess if your child can interpret information and data. Your child should be able to apply her or his understanding of growth to this example.

Total 6 marks

18 a Ticks in the correct boxes for:
living: duck, tree
non-living: tractor, barn
Award one mark for each correctly ticked box
No marks are awarded if both boxes are ticked   *4 marks*

b breath; reproduce; grow
   Any two answers: one mark each   *2 marks*

Note to Parent

Movement is not included as the tractor is able to move.

Total 6 marks

19 a The duck on the right with its south pole uppermost   *1 mark*
     b iron   *1 mark*

Note to Parent

This question assesses whether your child has a knowledge of the behaviour of magnets (unlike poles attract, like poles repel) and of materials which are magnetic and non-magnetic.

Total 2 marks

20 metal; heat; burn   *1 mark each*

Note to Parent

This question tests an understanding of materials and the properties that make them suitable for particular uses.

Total 3 marks

21 a Jane's battery is running down
        Jane's house has more lamps
        Jane has different lamps
        Any two answers: one mark each   *2 marks*
     b two   *1 mark*
     c two   *1 mark*

Note to Parent

This question is assessing whether your child can link cause and effect. Children can experiment with electricity at home cheaply and safely. Commercial kits are often expensive but a few pounds can buy a range of components including batteries, lamps, a motor and wire.

Total 4 marks

22 hard: iron nail, rock
     bendy: newspaper, plastic bags
     Award one mark for each correct answer.   *4 marks*

Note to Parent

Your child should be able to group materials according to their properties, such as hardness and flexibility. As your child plays with different materials you could encourage him or her to group materials according to their properties.

Total 4 marks

23 a The arrow should be drawn to the right   *1 mark*
     b it slows down   *1 mark*
     c made the ball flat on one side   *1 mark*

Note to Parent

This question assess an understanding of forces and their effects on objects.

Total 3 marks

24 a It has a strong foot *or* a firm grip so it is not swept away by the tide.   *1 mark*

    b young limpets have not reached the pool *or*
      there is no food *or* the pool is polluted
      Any one answer   *1 mark*

Note to Parent

This question assesses your child's ability to identify ways in which an animal is suited to its environment.

Total 2 marks

25 a is strong and will keep its shape.   b is easily shaped.   c is squashy.   *1 mark each*

Note to Parent

This question should encourage your child to think of the reason why certain materials are used for certain jobs. There is more than one possible answer in each case, but it is necessary for your child to select the correct reason in his or her answer.

Total 3 marks

26 a The biscuit mixture was put in a hot oven.   b melted   *1 mark each*

    c can change back: ice cubes cannot change back: cakes, bricks
      Award one mark for each correct answer; no marks if both boxes are ticked   *3 marks*

Note to Parent

It is important that your child realises that some changes can be reversed and others cannot.

Total 5 marks

27 a C   b C   c There are two batteries in the circuit.   1 mark each
                                                             Total 3 marks

28 a John   *1 mark*
    b John is nearer. The sound is quieter further away from the whistle   *2 marks*

Note to Parent

In part **b** there is a mark for simply saying John is nearer, but your child must show he or she understands that sound gets fainter further from its source for the second mark.

Total 3 marks

29 a push   *1 mark*
    b changes its shape and slows it down   *1 mark each*
                                                           Total 3 marks

30 iron, strong   *1 mark*
    plastic, can be moulded   *1 mark*
    gold, shiny   *1 mark*
                                                           Total 3 marks

31 a 3   *1 mark*
    b One wire from the end of the battery to the first bulb, one from the first bulb to the
      second bulb, and one from the second bulb to the other end of the battery.   *1 mark*
    c a second battery   *1 mark*

Note to Parent

If your child gives 4 as the answer to part **a** and then joins each bulb to the battery using two wires for each, she or he can gain the mark for part **b** but not **a**.

Total 3 marks

MARKING GRID

Question	Marks available	Marks scored
1	4	
2	3	
3	3	
4	8	
5	4	
6	3	
7	5	
8	9	
9	4	
10	2	
11	3	
12	3	
13	6	
14	4	
15	4	
Total	65	

Question	Marks available	Marks scored
16	6	
17	6	
18	6	
19	2	
20	3	
21	4	
22	4	
23	3	
24	2	
25	3	
26	5	
27	3	
28	3	
29	3	
30	3	
31	3	
Total	59	